The Blue crew

DUNE BUGGY FOR TWO

Written by Danny Munck
Illustrations by Ilya T

Sitting around the breakfast table
I'm wondering what this summer might hold.
Dad has been making big plans
and they are about to unfold.

He wants to build a dune buggy
and he's found an old parts car.
He needs my help to go get it
From down the road not that far.

INRI

We head down the road
looking to make a deal.
The car has been wrecked
and we get it for a steal.

We use the tools from our
handy tool cart.
With a spit and a sputter
we get the engine to start.

We take out the axle, engine
and transmission.
A project this big takes
lots of ambition.

Next its time to
start on the frame.
A two seat buggy
is the name of the game.

Now its time for
the paint job in blue.
Dad sprays on a basecoat
and clearcoat too.

We dress up the engine
while the blue paint dries.
This shiny new chrome
could sure win first prize.

We bolt in the parts
from the old parts car,
and fill up the brake fluid reservoir.

Tires and seats are
next in the queue.
Then set the timing
and adjust the air screw.

Only two things left
before the first test drive.
Buckle up your seatbelt,
and give Dad a high five!

Man this buggy is really fast!
Mom looks worried
as we go zipping past.

We zoom up and down
the hill in our yard.
We find a few bumps
and my teeth get jarred.

We add an American flag
just for show.
Dad says the buggy is ready to go.

Now onto the trailer
that's hooked to the truck,
and off to the sand dunes to run amuck.

Unload the buggy and
warm the engine up.
With the new paddle tires
we'll never get stuck.

There is endless fun on our
toy made for sand;
climbing big hills
just as we planned.

Twisting and turning with
whoops and big jumps!
The thrill of the ride
gives me loads of goosebumps.

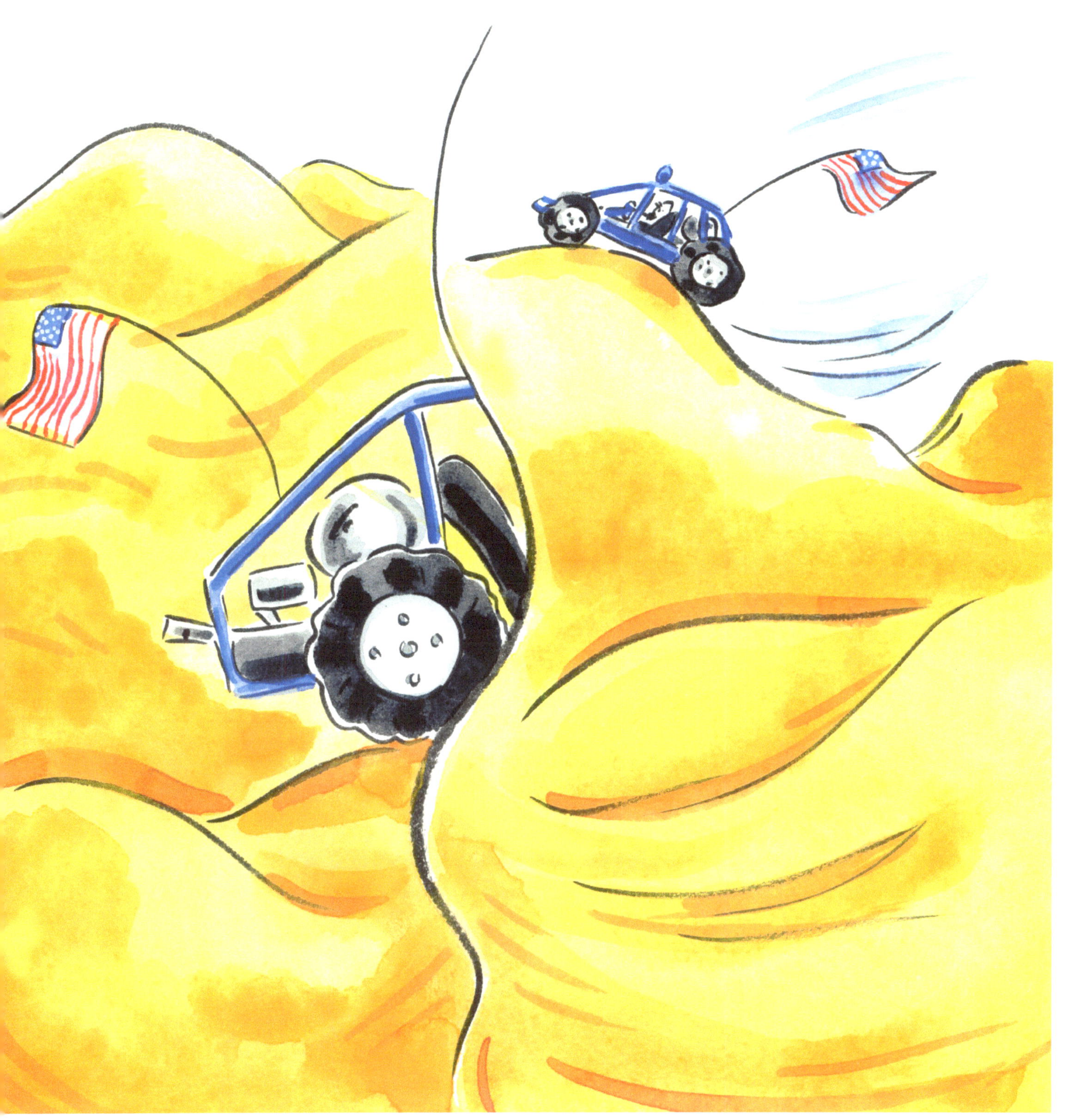

We do a big wheelie
after Dad dumps the clutch.
I let out a yelp
because it scares me so much.

Dad turns and says "Thank you, son!
With all your help it sure was fun."
He gives me a wink and we
crank up some tunes,
and take off like a rocket
back into the dunes.

www.ingramcontent.com/pod-product-compliance
Lightning Source LLC
LaVergne TN
LVHW071211160826
845679LV00003B/800

9798218980467